The Right Degree for Me™

WHAT DEGREE DO I NEED TO PURSUE A CAREER IN NURSING?

LINDA BICKERSTAFF

ROSEN PUBLISHING®

Published in 2015 by The Rosen Publishing Group, Inc.
29 East 21st Street, New York, NY 10010

Library of Congress Cataloging-in-Publication Data

Bickerstaff, Linda, author.
What degree do I need to pursue a career in nursing?/Linda
Bickerstaff.—First edition.
        pages cm.—(The right degree for me)
Audience: Grades 7–12.
Includes bibliographical references and index.
ISBN 978-1-4777-7857-9 (library bound)
1. Nursing—Vocational guidance—Juvenile literature. 2. Nurses—Juvenile
literature. I. Title.
RT82.B53 2015
610.73—dc23

                                                    2014006849

Manufactured in the United States of America

CONTENTS

INTRODUCTION

Recent information from the Bureau of Labor Statistics (BLS) reports that there are approximately 2.7 million registered nurses (RNs) in the United States. They, along with 736,400 licensed practical or vocational nurses (LPNs or LVNs) and 1.5 million certified nursing assistants (CNAs), constitute the largest group of health care providers in the United States. The jobs that these 4.9 million people do are numerous and varied, but all involve caring for others.

In a speech delivered to the American Nurses Association (ANA), President Barack Obama said, "America's nurses are the beating heart of our medical system." Although he was speaking to an association of RNs, his definition certainly applies to all members of the nursing profession.

President Obama was speaking of LPNs such as Jerry Avant Jr. After serving ten years in the U.S. Coast Guard, Avant became an LPN and was studying to become an RN. He was at work at the Pinelake Health and Rehabilitation Center in Carthage, North Carolina, when a gunman broke into the facility and began firing at patients and staff alike. In an attempt to shield his patients from harm, Avant was shot

Nursing is an art, an art of caring. Almost five million CNAs, LPNs, and RNs, one of whom is pictured here, demonstrate this art on a daily basis.

multiple times. He and seven others died of their wounds.

President Obama was also speaking of nurses such as Major General Patricia Horocho who are among the nation's leaders. Horocho is the first woman and the first nurse to serve as Army Surgeon General. She is a certified clinical trauma nurse whose training and skills were life-saving for many of those injured when terrorists flew a Boeing 757 into the Pentagon on September 11, 2001.

The nursing profession needs people with a wide variety of skills and interests. It needs nursing assistants and LPNs to provide basic, hands-on nursing care to patients in a variety of settings. It also needs registered nurses and nurse specialists to provide the highly complex care needed in operating rooms, emergency rooms, and intensive-care units. Many certificates and degrees can be earned to prepare nurses for all of these activities. They include CNA and LPN certificates, diplomas in nursing, associate's degrees in nursing (ADN) and bachelor of science degrees (BSN) in nursing. Master's and doctoral degrees can also be earned in nursing.

Nurses are in short supply, and the shortage will become greater in the years to come. Schools of nursing are expanding the number and scope of the courses they provide in an attempt to address this shortage. Men, for whom nursing is considered a nontraditional profession, are being encouraged to pursue nursing careers. Many large health care centers and numerous government agencies are offering financial assistance to nursing students. Teens who have a desire to help others and who want careers in a profession that offers a wide variety of jobs, above-average salaries, and excellent opportunities for advancement should consider nursing as a profession.

CHAPTER ONE

Nursing in a Nutshell

Nursing is a complex and multifaceted profession. Many people have tried to define the concept of nursing, but no single definition has prevailed. The definition proposed by the International Council of Nurses (ICN), as disclosed on its website, is accepted by professionals and patients alike. The Council says: "Nursing includes the promotion of health, prevention of disease, and the care of ill, disabled, and dying patients." Another definition of nursing, which is simple and heartfelt, was proposed by Kimberly Stults and published in the 2001 fall issue of the *Journal of Undergraduate Nursing.* She says: "Nursing is an

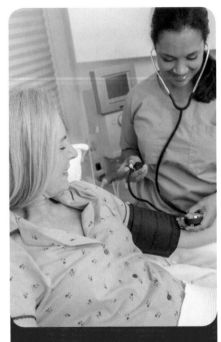

Checking a patient's blood pressure, as demonstrated here, is one of many skills used by nurses at all levels of training.

art, an art of caring." Registered nurses, licensed practical nurses, and certified nursing assistants are the people who practice this art of caring.

Paths to a Nursing Career

Although the book was written before today's teenagers were born, many teens have read and enjoyed Jean Auel's *The Clan of the Cave Bear.* Ayla, the heroine of this novel, is an adopted member of an imaginary prehistoric clan of people. The book tells of her transformation from outcast to the clan's healer. Ayla could well represent the first nurse because the practice of nursing dates to prehistoric times. The profession of nursing, on the other hand, is relatively new. Nursing professionals include certified nursing assistants, licensed practical nurses, and registered nurses. Working together as a team, they provide very sophisticated care for those who cannot care for themselves. What does each of these professionals do and how do they train for their jobs?

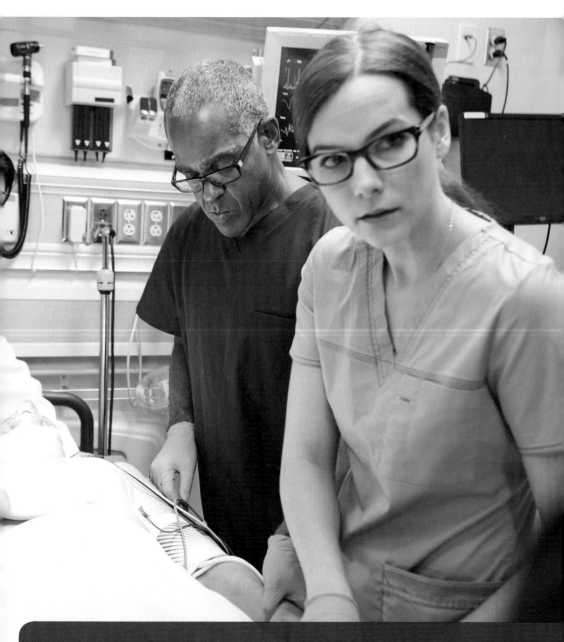

Nurses are a vital part of the team caring for the critically injured and ill in emergency rooms and ICUs.

Certified Nursing Assistant. Certified nursing assistants (CNAs) make up about 1.5 million of people working in nursing today. They provide the hands-on, day-to-day care for patients in nursing homes and other long-term care facilities, as well as in hospitals. They are not required to hold college degrees to practice. Training programs for nursing assistants last between four and twelve weeks. These programs include a minimum of seventy-five hours of classroom instruction and clinical training in an affiliated hospital, nursing home, or other facility. After successfully completing the training, a nursing assistant is eligible to take a competency examination to become a certified nursing assistant.

Licensed Practical/Vocational Nurse. Licensed practical nurses (LPNs) have more extensive training than CNAs, but also provide the basic nursing care needed by patients in a variety of settings. They also supervise CNAs in some facilities. LPNs are called licensed vocational nurses in the states of Texas and California. LPNs do not need college degrees to practice. LPN training programs are usually offered by community or vocational-technical colleges ("vo-techs"). The courses take between seven and twenty-four months to complete. These programs provide classroom or online classes and are affiliated with facilities where hands-on clinical experience is obtained. A certificate is awarded when the course is successfully completed. To practice, LPNs must take and pass the National Council Licensure Examination for Practical Nurses (NCLEX-PN).

Registered Nurse. Registered nurses (RNs) give more complex and specialized care than do CNAs and LPNs. There are three pathways to becoming an RN. Until the mid-1960s, most nurses trained in two-year hospital-based diploma programs. Today, there are fewer than forty of these programs still operating in the United States. Slightly more than half of the people now training to be registered nurses do so in associate's degree programs, which require two to three years to complete and are offered at community colleges or vo-techs. A bachelor of science degree in nursing usually requires four years to complete. This degree includes more training in the physical and social sciences and the humanities than do diploma or associate's degrees. Regardless of where they train, registered nurses must pass the NCLEX-RN examination before they can apply for licenses.

There are more than two hundred recognized subspecialties that nurses

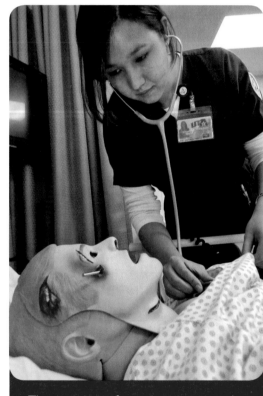

The training of nursing personnel involves the use of simulated patients, as indicated by the grievously traumatized mannequin pictured here.

can pursue. Some of these require nurses to obtain master's or doctorate degrees. Most simply require nurses to choose work opportunities that fit their areas of greatest interest.

Personality Traits for Nurses

Is a career in nursing a "good fit" for everyone? Absolutely not! Before considering nursing careers, teens should compare their own personality traits to those that career counselors and other professionals know are essential for happy, successful nurses. Five of the traits mentioned in an article on RN Builder (http://www.rnbuilder.com) are listed here:

1. Nurses are *caring* people who have both empathy and compassion.
2. Nurses are *detail-oriented* and able to focus while multitasking.
3. Nurses are *emotionally strong* and able to handle heartbreaking and devastating work.
4. Nurses have *great communication skills.*
5. Nurses are *flexible* and have the ability to adjust to changing conditions swiftly and competently.

Other experts on nursing personalities would add *patience*, *diligence*, and *diplomacy* to this list.

Men in Nursing Careers

Prior to the American Civil War, most of the nurses in the United States were men. When the Civil War began in 1861, it was obvious that many nurses would be needed to care for the sick and wounded. Male nurses cared for the wounded in the field. Female nurses cared for soldiers who were lucky enough to make it to hospitals alive. More than twenty thousand men and women provided nursing care for soldiers during that war.

In 1873, the New York Training School at Bellevue Hospital in New York City; the Connecticut Training School in New Haven, Connecticut; and the Boston Training School at Massachusetts General Hospital opened their doors for training of nurses. These programs excluded men. In spite of the establishment of nursing schools for men, such as the Mills School of Nursing and St. Vincent's Hospital School for Men in New York City, the number of male nurses dwindled. By 1930, they made up only 1 percent of the country's nurses.

In a CBS News article citing data from the U.S. Census Bureau, Ryan Jaslow reports that in 1970, men made up 2.7 percent of registered nurses. In 2011, almost 10 percent of employed RNs in the United States were men—about 330,000 men in total. The number of male LPNs also increased over that period. In 2011, 8.1 percent of LPNs were men. Some of the reasons the number of male nurses tripled since 1970 include the intensified recruiting efforts geared toward men, increased job opportunities in the nursing field, and reasonably high average salaries.

Nursing schools are developing strategies to attract and retain more male nursing students. Many of the programs emphasize that nurses, regardless of gender, must be tough to deal with the physical and emotional

Nursing is considered a nontraditional career for men, but that may soon change. The number of male nurses has tripled since 1970.

demands of the profession. An example of one of these strategies is an advertisement produced by the Oregon Center for Nursing in 2001. The center's advertising posters feature nine men and read: "These nine dudes are strong. They're tough. They're rugged. They're not sissies. They ride Harleys and snowboards. They play basketball and rugby. They've served in the Army and the Navy. Oh, by the way, they also happen to be nurses. And they've got a question for you: 'Mister, are you man enough to be a nurse?'"

Sampling Nursing as a Career

There are many exciting opportunities for teens who want to "try out" nursing before deciding whether it is the right profession for them. By participating in one or more of these programs, teens can be more confident that they are making the right decision when choosing to pursue a nursing career.

Career days in nursing. University nursing programs, large medical complexes, and many other organizations

sponsor "career days" aimed at teens. Program participants are given the opportunity to get an inside view
of what nurses do. Speakers usually "tell it like it is."
They try to show all sides of nursing so that teens can
make informed decisions when considering nursing
as a career. One such program is the annual Nursing
Career Luncheon sponsored by Cedars-Sinai Health
Careers Academy. The academy's program includes
a series of talks by nurses, followed by lunch and a
hospital tour. Among other activities, the 125 students who participated in this program in 2010 put on
scrubs, hats, masks, and shoe covers to tour operating
rooms where nurse anesthetists explained and demonstrated the equipment they use.

Nursing camps. Nursing camps are programs of
varying lengths that try to inspire students to pursue
careers in nursing. One such program is the four-day
Jackrabbit Nurse Camp sponsored by South Dakota
State University. Hands-on demonstrations and simulation models are used to give participants realistic
experiences in various nursing procedures. The nurse
camp for teens is held at the Rapid City campus of
South Dakota State University in June each year. Participants are housed in university dormitories and eat
at university cafeterias.

Student internships. Student internship programs
give potential nursing students more extensive hands-
on experience in nursing than either career days or
nursing camps. For example, the Area Health Education Center of Southwest Oregon in Roseburg, Oregon,

WALT WHITMAN (1819–1892), POET AND NURSE

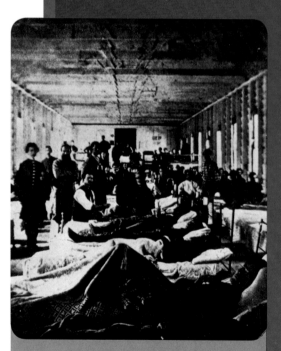

Walt Whitman worked in many hospitals similar to the one shown here during his career as a "psychological nurse" during the American Civil War.

Walt Whitman, who is best known as a journalist and poet, was forty-two years old when the American Civil War began in 1861. Too old to fight, he chose to help nurse the masses of sick and wounded soldiers the war generated. He is listed among the ten most famous male nurses in history in an article on BSN to MSN Online (http://bsntomsn.org). His initial contact with the war occurred when his younger brother, George, a Union soldier, was injured at the Battle of Fredericksburg in December 1862. Fearing the worst, Whitman searched many makeshift hospitals looking for him. He finally found George in a Falmouth, Virginia, hospital. George's hospital stay was short—he had only minor injuries. Walt, on the other hand, spent the remainder of the war in more than six hundred Union hospitals, serving as a volunteer nurse.

Whitman had no training as a nurse, but offered what help he could to the trained nurses and the doctors who cared for the physical ails of the sick and injured. Whitman felt that his major role was psychological nursing—giving moral support to the lonely, and often frightened, young soldiers in his care. These boys provided the inspiration for many of the poems Whitman wrote about his war experiences. "The Wound Dresser," written in 1867, is considered by many to celebrate the caring nature of nurses. The last verse of the poem contains these words:

"...The hurt and wounded I pacify with soothing hand.
I sit by the restless all the dark night,
Some are so young, some suffer so much.
I recall the experience sweet and sad..."

provides student internships in nursing. Teen interns participate in three ten-week site rotations during the high school academic year. They can earn up to six college credits that can be applied to programs at Oregon Health and Science University or other postsecondary programs that require community internship experience.

Teens can obtain lists of these opportunities from high school guidance counselors, from schools of nursing, from student nurse associations, or from the websites of sponsoring organizations.

CHAPTER TWO

Certified Nursing Assistants: Nursing's Front Line

I f a health care team could be compared to a football team, registered nurses and licensed practical nurses would be quarterbacks and running backs. CNAs would be linemen—the team members who receive "plays" from quarterbacks and then do the tough, basic work that keeps teams in the game. What do certified nursing assistants do and where do they work? Why would a person want to be a CNA? How can a person become a certified nursing assistant?

What? Where? Why?

CNAs are direct-care workers and spend more time with patients that any other members of the nursing team.

What CNAs do. Five of the most important duties that CNAs perform include:

1. Assisting patients with activities of daily living (ADL) in such a way that patients can retain their dignity. Activities of daily living are common everyday tasks, such as bathing or dressing, which a person must be able to perform to live independently.

CNAs, especially those working in home-health agencies, teach the activities of daily living needed to allow a patient to live independently.

2. Communicating with patients and their families and relaying important information gained during these discussions with other members of the care team.
3. Taking and recording patients' vital signs, such as heart rate, respiratory (breathing) rate, blood pressure, and temperature.
4. Monitoring patients' nutritional status and assisting in feeding patients if necessary.
5. Giving emotional support to patients and their families.

CNAs do many other tasks in the course of a day. Because they are team players, they join licensed nurses and registered nurses in doing whatever needs to be done to keep patients happy, safe, and as comfortable as possible.

Where CNAs work. According to the BLS, more than half of all CNAs work in long-term care facilities, such as nursing homes and rehab centers. The rest work in acute care hospitals, for home-health agencies, and in doctors' offices. As the number of long-term care facilities increases to meet the demands of the everaging population, many more nursing assistants will be needed to fill direct-care jobs. In 2010, there were about 1.5 million CNAs in the United States. It is

More than half of all CNAs work in nursing homes or rehabilitation centers caring for elderly and infirm people.

projected that by 2020, an additional three hundred thousand CNAs will be needed in the workforce.

Why CNAs work. Many people become CNAs as the first step in developing their careers in nursing. It only takes four to twelve weeks to complete the course work and obtain the clinical training needed to qualify to take credentialing exams. Once they are credentialed, CNAs can apply for jobs that pay enough and are flexible enough that they can study to become licensed or registered nurses.

Other nursing assistants spend their entire working years as CNAs because they love the caring nature of the work. Few, however, love the salaries they receive. New certified nursing assistants earn only slightly more than the minimum wage. Salaries do, however, increase as a person gains experience. Hospitals and home-health agencies usually pay higher wages than do long-term care facilities. Although salaries for CNAs are lower than those of licensed and registered nurses, CNAs are eligible for the same fringe benefits that the others receive. These may include health, dental, and life insurance, various retirement plans, and matching donations to individual retirement accounts. The BLS gives general information about salaries and compensation packages on its website. For specific and up-to-date information, consult PayScale (http://www.payscale.com) or Comp-Analysis (http://www.compensation.com) on the web.

How to Become a CNA

One of the positive aspects of becoming a CNA is that the training needed for the profession can be obtained quickly and in several different venues.

Prerequisites for CNA training. Prerequisites vary among training programs. Some of them are listed here:

1. Most programs require students to be at least eighteen years old.
2. Students must be able to read and speak English fluently.
3. Many training programs require students to have high school diplomas or GED certificates.
4. Students must have a physical examination and a TB tine test that screens for exposure to tuberculosis.
5. Students must undergo criminal background checks and be fingerprinted.

Length of training programs. Federal law dictates that CNAs acquire a minimum of seventy-five hours of training. Most states, however, require between 100 and 120 hours of training. Programs include both classroom and hands-on clinical training in which basic nursing skills are developed. The number of weeks needed to complete programs depends on the agency offering the training. For example, Wenatchee Valley College in Wenatchee, Washington, has two routes for completing CNA training. The first takes twelve weeks to complete. Classes meet for three hours, four days each week. The second is called the fast-track route and requires three weeks to complete. Classes meet for eight hours a day, five days every week.

Venues for CNA training. The five most common venues in which people train are technical or vocational high schools, community colleges or vo-tech colleges, hospitals or long-term care facilities, the

CNA courses require between 75 and 120 hours of training that include classroom work and hands-on clinical skills development.

U.S. Job Corps, or in American Red Cross programs. Online programs for CNAs are limited.

Cost of CNA training. CNA training can be obtained free of charge in several ways. Many long-term care facilities run training programs for their own employees. Employees are not charged for the courses and may be paid their regular salaries while taking them. The only expense these nursing assistants will encounter is the cost of taking the certification examination.

The U.S. Job Corps also provides CNA training at no charge to eligible students. Training in the Job Corps requires an eight-to-twelve month commitment. Cadets receive free room and

HOSA HONORS HERO

While in high school, Daniel Hernandez Jr. studied to become a CNA through a local chapter of Health Occupations Students of America (HOSA). An article by Scott Martindale for the *Orange County Register* describes why Hernandez received the Heroes Award by HOSA at its 2011 national conference in Santa Ana, California.

After graduating from high school with the intent of working in the field of nursing, Hernandez enrolled

President Barack Obama shakes hands with Daniel Hernandez, the CNA and congressional intern credited with saving the life of U.S. Representative Gabrielle Giffords.

at the University of Arizona to further his education. While there, his career goals switched from nursing to politics. As part of his course of study, he obtained a congressional internship to work for U.S. Representative Gabrielle Giffords of Arizona. He had been on the job five days when Giffords took her "Congress on Your Corner" program to a supermarket parking lot in Casas Adobes, Arizona. There, a gunman, intent on assassinating Giffords, opened fire, injuring thirteen people and killing six. Hernandez realized that Giffords was badly injured and, using skills he had learned as a CNA, elevated her head and applied pressure to her head wound. Both actions slowed the bleeding that threatened her life. After emergency medical personnel arrived to assume her care, he accompanied her to the hospital to provide emotional support until her family could be contacted. He is credited with saving her life.

After receiving HOSA's Heroes Award, presented by U.S. Surgeon General Regina Benjamin, Hernandez said, "I don't think I'm a hero. I think the people who make a lifetime commitment to helping others are the real heroes."

board and small stipends. Some vocational high schools also offer CNA training programs at no charge to high school students.

Community colleges and vo-techs charge fees similar to those charged for other courses of study.

The number of credit hours required for CNA certification varies from college to college, as does the tuition charged per credit hour. Current tuition rates can be obtained on the websites of most colleges. Expenses other than tuition usually include the costs of books, uniforms, shoes, and some equipment. Students must also pay credentialing exam fees. It is important for students to save receipts for all the expenses incurred during their training. If CNAs are employed within twelve months of completing their training by nursing homes that accept Medicaid patients or skilled nursing facilities that receive money from Medicare, their employers are required by federal law to reimburse them for most of the costs of their training.

American Red Cross–sponsored CNA training programs also charge fees. These vary depending on the city in which the programs are offered. Total costs may be as high as programs offered at community colleges, but good scholarships are frequently available to eligible students.

The Final Steps

After completing training, CNAs must pass certification examinations before they can be licensed to practice. The National Nurse Aide Assessment Program (NNAAP) is the exam given in most states. It has two parts. The first is a hands-on skills demonstration that is usually conducted in a nursing care facility. Students who pass part one of the exam take a computer-generated exam to complete their evaluations for certification. CNA practice exam study guides, practice exams, nurse aide skill videos, and various tutorials are available online to help candidates prepare for this exam.

CNAs who successfully complete their exams may apply for state licensure and begin their job searches if they are not already employed. CNAs are required to take continuing education courses to retain certification and licensure. The number of hours and types of courses vary from state to state. States dictate how often CNAs must renew their licenses.

CHAPTER THREE

Licensed Practical Nurses: Nursing's Tweens

n her article "10 Words Invented by Authors" for *Mental Floss* (http://www.mentalfloss.com), Stacy Conradt says, "In *The Fellowship of the Ring* [written by J. R. R. Tolkien in 1954] Tolkien claimed a Tween was a Hobbit between the ages of 20 and 33 (33 being when Hobbits come of age). There's some debate as to whether the word existed prior to this reference or not…" It is likely that the word was used long before the publication of *The Lord of the Rings* series. The word "tween" comes from the Middle-English word "twene," which is short for "betwene." The word is commonly used today to designate young people who are older than children but not yet teens—kids between the ages of nine and thirteen.

When used in the context of nursing and the jobs done by various people in the profession, licensed practical nurses are tweens. They come between nursing assistants and registered nurses in several ways: their training programs are longer than those of nursing assistants, but not as long as programs for registered nurses; they make more money than nursing assistants, but not as much as registered nurses. LPNs are direct caregivers, sharing hands-on, basic nursing duties with nursing assistants. They also have many duties that they share with RNs. In light of these overlaps, is there still a place for licensed practical nurses in the spectrum of health care providers? If teens commit to becoming LPNs, will there be jobs available when they finish their training? Nursing authorities strongly believe that

LPNs, shown here at their graduation ceremony, will face new and different challenges as their roles in the nursing profession change.

LPNs are critical to the nursing profession. Jobs are available for LPNs now and will continue to be plentiful. The nature of these jobs, however, is changing.

What? Where? Why?

The tasks that LPNs are licensed to undertake depend on the states in which they are licensed. Some states restrict the duties of licensed practical nurses to day-to-day nursing care similar to that provided by CNAs. Other states license LPNs to carry out almost all the duties of registered nurses. Teens interested in becoming LPNs should ascertain what they will be able to do in the state in which they want to practice before making a commitment to an LPN program.

What LPNs do. Like nursing assistants, LPNs perform basic bedside nursing duties. They assist patients in activities of daily living, take vital signs, communicate with patients and their families, and essentially do all the things that CNAs do. But they also perform many duties that CNAs are not trained to do. They assemble, use, and clean medical equipment and instruct patients in its use. They also place needles or catheters into patients' veins through which fluids and medications can be given. Unlike most CNAs, licensed practical nurses can dispense medications that have been ordered by physicians. They are trained to do complicated wound care, feed and otherwise care for babies in nurseries, supervise CNAs, and to do many other tasks.

Where LPNs work. The BLS reports that in 2010 there were about 750 thousand jobs for LPNs in the United States. It is anticipated that by 2020 there will be nine hundred thousand positions available. Twenty-nine percent of LPNs work in long-term care facilities. They are frequently the supervisors in nursing homes on evening and night shifts. Most of the rest work in acute care hospitals or in doctors' offices. Some also

An LPN takes a patient's health history. LPNs find many jobs in doctors' offices and clinics.

work for home-health agencies, in schools, or for other agencies, such as the American Red Cross.

Ben Casselman, a writer for the *Wall Street Journal*, reports on a study conducted by Burning Glass, a Boston-based company that analyzes workforce trends. That study showed that "licensed practical and vocational nurses are being pushed out of hospitals." Hospitals are now hiring more CNAs, whose salaries are lower than LPN salaries, to do hands-on nursing care. RNs now do many of the jobs, such as starting intravenous lines (IVs), which were previously done by LPNs. Most jobs for licensed nurses are now found in long-term care facilities, in outpatient clinics, or in doctors' offices.

Why LPNs work. LPNs, like nursing assistants and registered nurses, enter the profession because they want to care for others. Some LPNs began their nursing careers as CNAs. They choose to get additional education to improve their opportunities for advancement and find jobs with higher salaries. Many others, however, become LPNs to make money while studying to be RNs. According to Jane Zaccardi, director of Health Occupations and Practical Nursing at Johnson County Community College in Overland Park, Kansas, "Seventy-five to eighty percent of [LPN] students plan to go on to higher education."

Salaries for LPNs vary by the number of years they have worked, for whom they are working, and the geographic location of their jobs. Starting salaries are not much greater than those of CNAs, but salaries increase more rapidly as a person gains experience. A career LPN who has worked twenty years or more will make almost double the salary of a career CNA and about 80 percent of the salary of an RN with equal experience. Current salaries in the profession can be reviewed on PayScale (http://www.payscale.com) or other online sites.

How to Become an LPN

As with CNAs, a person can obtain training to become an LPN in several ways. Many programs are structured to accommodate people who are working part-time to help pay for their educations. Detailed information about LPN programs can be obtained at the website Licensed Practical Nurse (http://www.licensedpracticalnurse.net).

Prerequisites for LPN programs. Most LPN programs have a set of requirements that students must meet before admission. Almost all programs have the following requirements:

1. Students should be at least seventeen years old at the start of a program.
2. Students must have a high school diploma or GED certificate.
3. Students must pass criminal background checks and drug-screening tests. They must also have a physical examination and TB tine test for tuberculosis.
4. Many programs require students to take and pass examinations that test essential

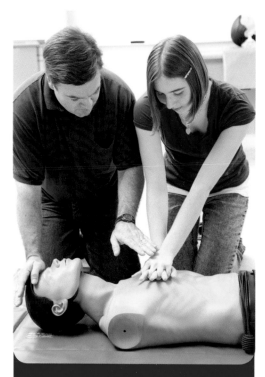

Cardiopulmonary resuscitation (CPR) certification is required to complete most LPN training programs. An instructor is shown assisting a student in learning techniques for this certification.

academic skills. The American College Test (ACT) is one such test. Another is the Test of Essential Academic Skills (TEAS).

5. Most programs insist that students have cardio-pulmonary resuscitation (CPR) certification, and some require students to be licensed CNAs.

Length and cost of training programs. LPN training programs are usually twelve to eighteen months long. Some accelerated courses can be completed in less than a year. There are LPN programs that will meet the scheduling needs of almost any person.

The cost of LPN programs depends mostly on the training venue. Training in the U.S. Job Corps costs nothing. The cost of other programs can be reviewed by going directly to the websites of the schools a person would be interested in attending. The BLS gives general guidelines about program costs, but more specific information can be obtained from the National Center for Education Statistics at http://nces.ed.gov.

Venues for LPN training. The training venues most commonly used by those wishing to become LPNs are: online programs; programs at vocational high schools; programs in community colleges, vo-techs, and universities; and programs with the U.S. Job Corps.

Online programs should be accredited by the National League of Nursing Accrediting Commission (NLNAC). This accreditation assures that the program meets at least minimal standards for LPN programs and qualifies graduates to take the NCLEX-PN exam. Online programs provide flexibility—a student chooses the time and place to take the course. Online programs may or may not be affiliated with institutions where students can get the clinical experience they need. A person must be a self-starter to get the most out of online courses and have computer equipment and the ability to use it well.

There are many vocational high schools across the country. LPN courses in these high schools are usually considered to be

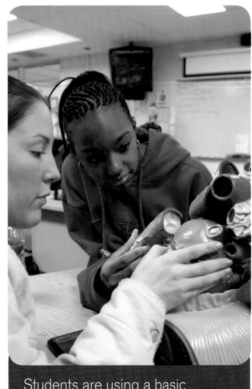

Students are using a basic anatomic model of a human heart to enhance their knowledge in a nursing class. Online LPN training courses must be combined with hands-on clinical experience.

postgraduate-level courses, and tuition is charged to take them. For instance, Willoughby-Eastlake School of Practical Nursing in Eastlake, Ohio, is part of the regional high school system. High school students enter the LPN program in their junior year, although they have to have completed almost all the courses needed for high school graduation before starting the LPN course. The tuition and all fees for the course are about the same for similar courses in community colleges and vo-techs. When students complete the course, they are eligible to take the licensing exam in Ohio and receive their high school diplomas. They can jump straight from high school into the nursing workforce.

Many community colleges and vo-techs also offer LPN courses. Most offer the option of taking courses full-time during the day and completing the course within ten to twelve months, or taking an evening/weekend program that requires about twenty-four months to complete. The curriculum is the same for both courses.

Universities also have LPN programs. Pennsylvania University's program is an eighteen-month-long, non-credit program leading to a certificate in practical nursing. This course is structured for night and weekend classes, so it can be taken by people who are working.

The U.S. Job Corps offers training leading to an LPN degree. This course is eight to fourteen months long. Students receive room and board and a small stipend during training. Most Job Corps positions are reserved for students from low-income families.

HOW LUCKY CAN YOU GET?

Training to become an LPN is one of the fastest ways to get started in a nursing career. Some people are actually lucky enough to get paid while getting their LPN credentials. Does it sound too good to be true? Well, it isn't. Just ask LPN students at the Cassadaga Job Corps Center in Cassadaga, New York. These lucky young people are enrolled in both a U.S. Job Corps advanced training program and a New York State–approved adult education course. When they finish the course, they will take the NCLEX-PN exam at no charge to themselves and will be assisted in finding jobs as LPNs. Some might even be sent to nearby Jamestown Community College to begin work toward their RN degrees. Students receive bi-weekly stipends, medical, dental and vision care, three meals a day, uniforms, and books. They also have access to a great recreational facility in which to exercise and play. They are housed in dorms that are posh by college standards. What do they have to do to qualify for this great deal? They must be high school graduates or have GED certificates. They must take the Test of Adult Basic Education (TABE) and make a score of six hundred or more. They need to have strong work histories and be highly recommended by teachers and employers. They must also come from low-income families who could not typically afford to send them to college. Cassadaga is just one of many Job Corps centers that provides this phenomenal opportunity. If you think you might qualify, check out the website http://recruiting.jobcorps.gov for a list of centers that offer LPN training. You could be one of the lucky ones!

Wrapping It Up

The last step a future LPN must take is to apply for and pass an examination that tests his or her ability to perform the job. The National Council of State Boards of Nursing (NCSBN) developed a computer-assisted exam, NCLEX-PN, to standardize this process. Students who pass this exam can then apply for licensure in the state where they want to work. Most states require an LPN to renew his or her license every two to four years. Most also require the person to take continuing education courses before applying for license renewal.

LPNs who decide in the future to become RNs or to earn a bachelor's degree may get credit for LPN coursework. LPNs with work experience may also be able to "test out" of certain classes. Both possibilities will save LPNs time and money in pursuing their advanced degrees.

CHAPTER FOUR

Registered Nurses: The Top of the Heap

Most teens have heard of Florence Nightingale, the British nurse credited with founding today's nursing profession, and Clara Barton, the founder of the American Red Cross. They are also likely to know that nurse Rory Williams, a character in the British science fiction TV series *Doctor Who*, carried important medical supplies during his time travels and that nurse Carla Espinosa was the spunky head nurse at the Sacred Heart teaching hospital portrayed in the American TV comedy-drama *Scrubs*. It is no surprise to them that registered nurses are found at the pinnacle of the nursing profession. Teens may not know, however, that registered nurses are the most numerous of professional health care providers. They make the most money of any nursing professional; they have the most flexibility in choosing the jobs they will do; and, according to the BLS, registered nurses have more job security than professionals in any field.

Teens considering nursing as a profession should know that there are three pathways from which to choose: obtaining a diploma in nursing from a hospital-based nursing program; obtaining an associate's degree in nursing from programs in community and vocational colleges; or earning a bachelor of science degree in nursing from a four-year college or university. The core curriculum in nursing that a person studies in any of these programs is the same. The programs differ only in what the prerequisites are for taking them, the time it takes to complete them, how much it costs to take them, and what additional education is obtained along the way. To some extent, the jobs that will be available at the end of training also vary according to the educational pathway an individual takes.

Core Knowledge in Nursing

What core knowledge do all registered nurses need? Nurses themselves, working through their various associations and governing bodies, decided what core knowledge they needed to obtain in training programs to work safely, effectively, and compassionately. Core subject matter in most nursing programs can be broken down into four general categories. The categories and some of the topics covered within the categories are listed below.

1. **Issues in Nursing Practice.** Topics covered include the history of nursing and the theories and skills that are essential to the profession. Students are introduced to the concepts of critical thinking, decision making, legal and ethical issues in nursing, and how economic factors affect nursing.

2. **Human Pathophysiology.** Classes in this category cover how illnesses affect human bodies. The emphasis is on understanding the commonality in a variety of diseases and the relationship of diseases and the signs and symptoms they produce.
3. **Nursing Pharmacology.** In pharmacology classes, students learn about commonly used drugs and how they influence body systems. Ethical and legal issues related to prescription drugs are also discussed.

One part of the core curriculum for RN students is nursing pharmacology. Students pictured here listen to a lecture on the effects of various medications on body systems.

4. Health Assessment. Classes in this category teach the skills needed to evaluate how all the parts of the body work. All body systems, from the heart to the brain to the skin, produce signs that indicate if they are functioning normally or not. Students learn normal vital signs and how the signs change in various disease states. Students also learn interviewing techniques so that they can take good medical histories from their patients.

The National Council of State Boards of Nursing developed the National Council Licensure Examination for Registered Nurses (NCLEX-RN). RN candidates take this exam at the end of their training programs to prove that they have good command of the core knowledge needed in nursing. NCSBN provides an extensive discussion of the makeup of NCLEX-RN on http://www.ncsbn.org. There are also several websites that provide sample examinations that prospective RNs can study.

Pathways to RN Licensure

Students can take one of three pathways to qualify as registered nurses.

Diploma in nursing. Until the early 1960s, most RNs received their training in one of almost 1,300 hospital-based schools of nursing located throughout the United States. In the course of their training, nursing students provided most of the nursing care for patients in the

NURSES SING, TOO!

It is a little-known fact that there are many acclaimed actors, actresses, and singers that are also registered nurses. An article on the blog *Accelerated Nursing* (http://acceleratednursing.net) lists ten of these nurses along with short biographies of each. Naomi Judd is one person who is featured in the article. According to the website for Academy of Achievement (http://achievement.org), Judd, a single mother of two daughters, was thirty years old when she finally saved enough money to go to college. She attended the College of Marin, a community college in California, where she earned an associate's degree in nursing. She subsequently worked as a nurse in the intensive care unit (ICU) of a hospital in Franklin, Tennessee. A patient she had cared for in the ICU heard Naomi and her daughter, Wynonna, sing. He was so impressed that he secured an audition with RCA Records for them. The rest is history. The duo, known as The Judds, was soon on its way to stardom. They went on to win five Grammy Awards over the years that they sang together. In 1991, Naomi fell ill and was diagnosed with hepatitis C, a viral disease that affects the liver. It is probable that she acquired the virus from a needle-stick injury that occurred when she was working in the ICU. Fortunately, Naomi experienced a remission from the disease and is now working as a spokesperson for the American Liver Foundation. She has underwritten the Naomi Judd Education and Research Foundation to raise awareness of the deadly hepatitis C virus.

hospitals in which they trained. At completion of the programs, nurses earned diplomas rather than degrees in nursing. State boards of nursing began credentialing nursing schools in the 1960s. To be credentialed, a nursing school could not use nursing students as unpaid nursing personnel. Because of this restriction, many nursing schools became financial liabilities to hospitals and were closed. The forty

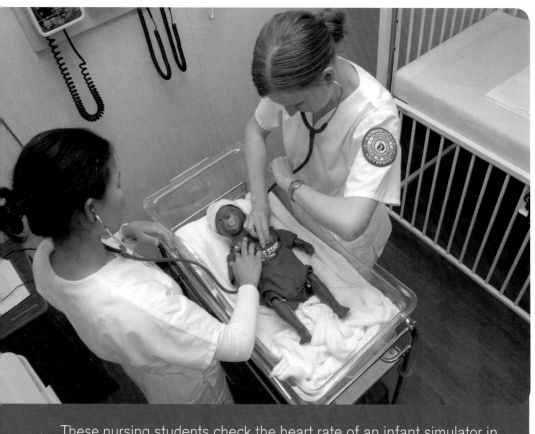

These nursing students check the heart rate of an infant simulator in a nursing simulation laboratory at their college. Nursing students must learn to care for patients of all ages.

remaining hospital-based nursing programs now train about 4 percent of all registered nurses.

Diploma programs usually take two to three years to complete. The emphasis of these programs is on teaching core nursing material in a clinical setting. Although being very skilled in clinical nursing, diploma nurses usually don't receive the "book learning" needed to get more advance, higher-paying nursing jobs.

The cost of the programs ranges widely depending on what is included in the costs and the length of the programs. In general, diploma programs are less expensive than other nursing degree programs. To get current information on the cost of these programs, go directly to the websites of hospitals offering diploma nursing programs. Many hospitals offer scholarships that can help with expenses. Some will waive tuition and fees entirely if graduates of the program commit to working in the training hospital for a set length of time after graduation.

Associate's degree in nursing. Associate's degrees in nursing (ADN) are offered at community colleges, vo-techs, and at some state and private universities. The programs are usually two years long. If prerequisite courses are factored into the time needed to complete the course, it is likely that three years will be needed. Many ADN courses are "blended" courses in which students do classroom work online while getting clinical training at designated clinical facilities. Blended courses require students to have very good study habits, a lot of self-discipline, and good computer equipment and skills. The advantage of blended courses is that the online work can be done from a student's home at a time that is convenient for him or her. This flexibility is especially helpful for those who must work.

ADN programs offered at community colleges and vo-techs are usually less expensive than those completed in four-year colleges or universities because per-credit tuition rates are usually lower in community colleges and vo-techs. For example, data from the National Center for Education Statistics shows that an associate's degree nursing program at the University of Wisconsin-Madison, a state university, charges 2.7 times as much in tuition each year as is charged at Madison Technical College, a vo-tech. Tuition for a similar course at Concordia University, a private, church-affiliated university in Mequon, Wisconsin, is 6.5 times as much as at Madison Technical College.

Bachelor of science in nursing. Data from "Charting Nursing's Future," an article from the Robert Wood Johnson Foundation, shows that in 2013, only 4 percent of nurses trained in diploma programs, while 53 percent trained in ADN programs and 43 percent in BSN programs. It is anticipated that by 2020, at least three-quarters of nurses will have bachelor's degrees and many will have master's or doctorate degrees in nursing. The need for more highly trained RNs is fueled partially by changes in the profession itself. Maureen Wallace, Ed.D., RN, a faculty fellow in the Office of the Dean of Health and Human Services at City University of New York, says:

"Most ADN students get excellent clinical experience, but their education has been heavily skills-oriented and focused on acute care. Much of health care going forward will be about prevention, patient education, and helping patients gain access to resources in the community—competencies acquired at the BSN level."

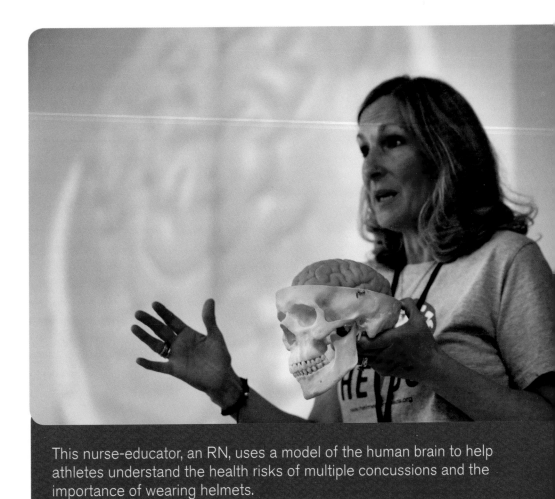

This nurse-educator, an RN, uses a model of the human brain to help athletes understand the health risks of multiple concussions and the importance of wearing helmets.

Students who are considering nursing as a career should give strong consideration to pursing a BSN degree directly, rather than obtaining a diploma in nursing or an ADN degree. Three states—New York,

A mother helps her daughter *(left)*, a senior nursing student, review the options for financial aid. Because of the increasing complexity of the nursing profession, all RNs may eventually be required to have at least BSN degrees, which will affect the financial decisions of families.

New Jersey, and Rhode Island—have introduced legislation that would require all registered nurses in those states to earn BSN degrees within ten years of their initial licensing. Whether or not state governments should legislate degrees in nursing is a controversial issue among nurses and nursing associations, but it may be the wave of the future.

BSN programs usually require four years to complete. The costs of these courses vary with the college or university offering them and reflect variability in the tuition charged at these schools. The U.S. Department of Education's National Center for Education Statistics offers a wealth of information on tuition costs at colleges and universities in the United States on its website (http://nces.ed.gov). The College Affordability and Transparency Center at that site compares the cost of BSN programs among several different colleges and universities across the country.

Needless to say, getting a BSN degree, like any college degree, is an expensive undertaking. The upside is that most nurses with BSN degrees can find good jobs in a relative short period of time. American Association of Colleges of Nursing (AACN) (http://www.aacn.nche.edu) reports on a survey conducted by the AACN in 2011. The purpose of the survey was to find out how well nurses with a new BSN degree fared on the job market. Fifty-six percent of BSN graduates found jobs immediately after receiving their licenses. This number compared with a 24 percent employment rate for new college graduates across disciplines. Eighty-eight percent of BSN nurses found jobs within four to six months after receiving their licenses.

CHAPTER FIVE

The Sky's the Limit . . . or Is It?

he common phrase "The sky's the limit" can be used to imply that a person has almost limitless possibilities in his or her career choices. That is certainly the case in nursing. Nursing careers can extend beyond the sky into the far reaches of space or into specialty areas that are applicable to undersea exploration. With more than two hundred specialties from which to choose, every nurse can find the perfect job. Many of the most interesting and challenging jobs, however, require nurses to have at least a bachelor of science in nursing (BSN) degree. Others require a master's degree (MSN) or doctorate in nursing. Advanced practice registered nurses (APRNs) are already required to have a master's degree in nursing along with certificates in their specialty areas. These nurses practice as clinical nurse specialists, nurse practitioners, nurse midwives, and nurse anesthetists.

Most new registered nurses aren't thinking about advanced degrees, however. They have one thing in mind—getting a job to earn the money to repay college debts. They would love to get a higher degree, but working is a necessity. Is there some way they can work toward a higher degree without actually returning to nursing school? How can they go back to school and still work? "Bridge" programs in nursing allow nurses to get a higher degree without physically returning to nursing school. They also allow nurses to work while advancing their education.

Bridge Programs to Higher Degrees

It is probable that by 2025, all RNs will need bachelor's degrees to be licensed to practice. The changing role of LPNs in nursing may also encourage many LPNs to become registered nurses. "Bridge" programs in nursing have been developed to facilitate moves from lower degrees to higher ones. Two of the most frequently used bridge programs allow licensed practical nurses to become registered nurses in ADN programs or obtain bachelor's degrees. Nurses who have obtained their registered nursing credentials in associate's degree programs may bridge to a bachelor's or master's degree. Nurses who already have their bachelor's degree can bridge to a master's degree relatively quickly. Many bridge programs allow nurses to do coursework online from their homes without stepping foot into a nursing school. Because nurses can do coursework at their convenience, they can continue to work while studying.

An example of an online bridge program in nursing is one offered at Western Governors University (WGU).

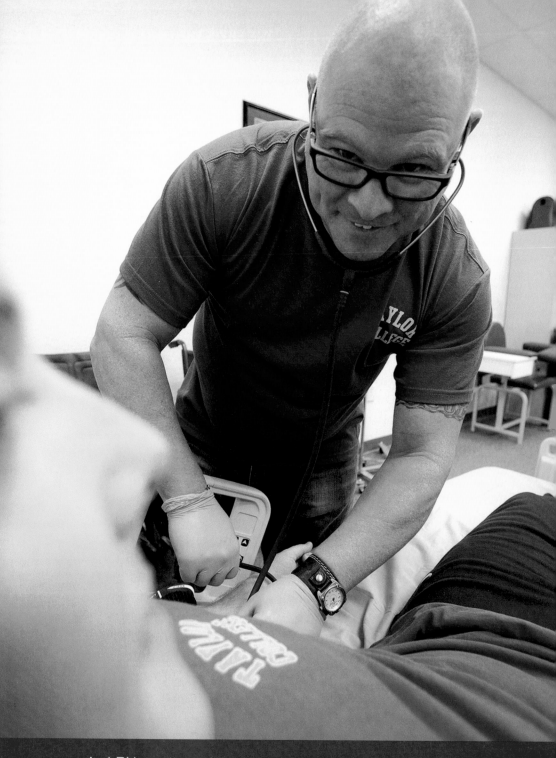

An LPN practices clinical skills in an online LPN to RN bridge program at Taylor College, in Belleville, Florida. The program required thirty-six credit hours of instruction.

WGU was founded by governors of nineteen western states and incorporated as a private, nonprofit university in 1997. It was created to expand access to higher education through online, competency-based degree programs. Its mission is to help hardworking adults meet their education goals and improve their career opportunities. The founding governors insisted that WGU be affordable, flexible, and student-focused. Because it is a nonprofit university, its tuition is among the lowest in the country. The university's RN to BSN program requires 120 competency units or credits to complete. Most nurses can transfer fifty hours of credit from the programs in which they received their registered nurse credentials. In addition to the clinical work an RN has already completed, this program requires a minimum of ninety hours of mentor-guided clinical experience in a qualified community health services setting, such as a public health clinic. Most nurses can complete this bridge program in eighteen months.

Master's and doctoral programs in nursing.
Master's degrees are now being required for many nurses who want to work in specialty areas. Nurses who are looking for leadership roles, faculty positions in universities, or research jobs need to acquire either a doctorate in nursing practice (DNP) or a Ph.D. degree. There are few, if any, bridge programs to doctorate or Ph.D. degrees in nursing. The doctorate of nursing practice is a practice-oriented doctorate, while the Ph.D. is a research-oriented degree. DNP degrees usually take five semesters

A SPECIALTY FOR EVERY NURSE

There are more than two hundred nursing subspecialties, many of which require nurses to complete specific courses of study to be certified in the field. Many of these programs lead to MSN degrees. Twenty of the more than two hundred nursing subspecialties are listed below:

Certified Neuroscience RN

Certified Post-Aesthesia RN

Adult Nurse Practitioner

Medical/Surgical RN

Cardiac/Vascular Surgery Nurse

Certified Flight Nurse

Certified Hospice and

Palliative Care RN

Neonatal RN

Wound and Ostomy Care RN

Nurse Researcher

Certified Gastroenterology RN

Legal Nurse Consultant

Certified Nurse Anesthetist

Pediatric RN

Nurse Executive

Operating Room Nurse

Certified Nephrology Nurse

Gerontology Nurse Practitioner

Orthopedic Nurse

Certified Nurse Midwife

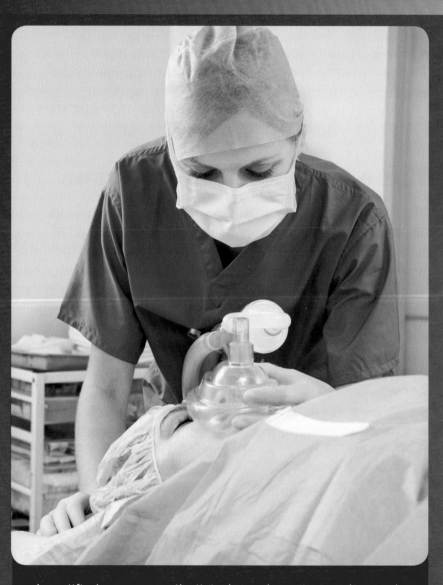

A certified nurse anesthetist, shown here, is an advanced practice nurse and is required to have at least a master's degree, as well as a special certificate in anesthesiology.

beyond the master's degree to complete. Ph.D.s in nursing usually take four to five years to complete. At the present time, advanced practice RNs can practice with master's degrees and specialty certifications, but it will soon be necessary for APRNs to have doctorate degrees to practice.

Three Far-Out Jobs for Nurses

Most people think of nurses as the women who take care of them when they are in the hospital, the people who direct the show at their doctors' offices, or scrubs-clad women giving flu shots at the local public health clinic. With more than two hundred specialties available to nurses, however, some of the jobs they do are really "far out."

Space nurse. The National Aeronautics and Space Administration (NASA) has never chosen a nurse to be an astronaut. That's not to say that nurses aren't actively involved in space nursing. Starting with Dee O'Hara, the nurse chosen to care for NASA's *Mercury 7* astronauts in 1959, nurses have worked as hands-on caregivers for astronauts and their families, as well as caring for other NASA personnel.

Other would-be space nurses are planning ahead to the time when prolonged space exploration by manned spacecraft begins. In 1991, a group of nurses founded the Space Nursing Society (SNS), an international space advocacy organization devoted to space nursing and the contribution to space exploration by nurses. The SNS provides a forum for the discussion and exploration of issues related to nursing in space. There are now more than four hundred members of this society. Members are developing educational programs and writing a textbook about nursing in space. They are also considering a future certification in space nursing. Information about the society can be obtained at its website (http://www.spacenursingsociety.net). Teens now considering careers in nursing will be finishing their educations about the time this nursing specialty becomes a reality.

Certified hyperbaric registered nurse (CHRN). Most scientists would agree that they know more about space than they know about the depth of the oceans. Just as there is a nursing specialty that concentrates on the nursing care of space travelers, there are also nurses whose specialty is applicable to the care of those who explore the ocean depths— certified hyperbaric registered nurses. Hyperbaric chambers are used to treat decompression sickness, more commonly known as the "bends," which is one of the hazards of underwater diving. The emphasis of the nursing care given by most CHRNs, however, is the use of hyperbaric oxygen treatment (HBOT) in the care of patients with a multitude of medical and surgical problems. Simply put, oxygen is needed for the proper functioning of all cells in humans. If cells don't get enough oxygen, they die. If a person is placed in a hyperbaric oxygen

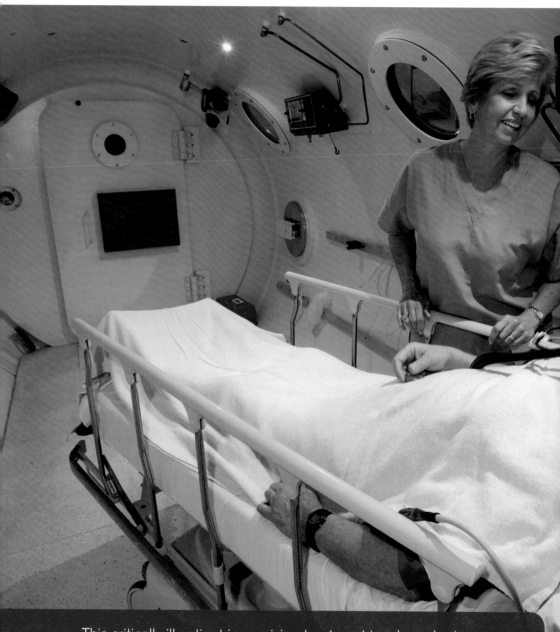

This critically ill patient is receiving treatment in a hyperbaric oxygen chamber. A certified hyperbaric registered nurse supervises his treatment.

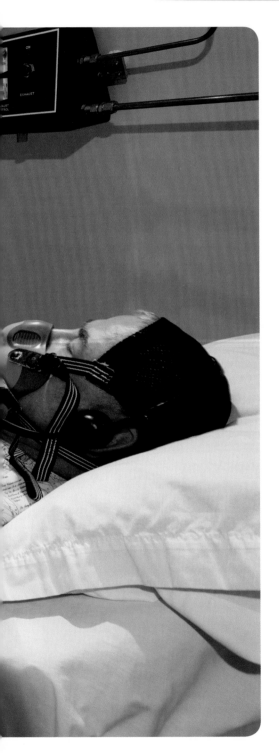

chamber, where he or she breaths 100 percent oxygen at a pressure greater than normal atmospheric pressure, oxygen is forced into body tissues. Cells that make up these tissues get the additional oxygen they need to survive and regenerate. One of the main applications of HBOT is in the treatment of complicated, non-healing skin ulcers and other types of wounds. HBOT is also being used to treat multiple sclerosis, Lyme disease, cerebral palsy, strokes, and other catastrophic illnesses.

Because patients with these problems are usually quite ill, nurses must be able to deal with many emergency situations. They must also be knowledgeable about the treatment method itself.

DEE O'HARA:
THE FIRST SPACE NURSE

A NASA Quest (http://quest.arc.nasa.gov) article tells the story of Dee O'Hara, who was an air force nurse at Patrick Air Force Base, Florida, in 1959. One day, she was asked if she would like to be an astronaut nurse for NASA Project Mercury. She says she was totally ignorant about NASA, Project Mercury, and who astronauts were, but she accepted the job anyway. She says, "It turned out I was to set up the Aeromed Lab, the exam area for the astronauts, and be with them as their nurse." Her job expanded to helping with preflight physical examinations just before astronauts were launched on their missions from Cape Canaveral, Florida. "I was always quite afraid every time they launched," she says. "It was like putting one of my best friends on a Roman candle."

To continue working in the space program, O'Hara resigned her air force commission and moved with the astronauts to Johnson Space Center in Houston in 1964. She worked with Gus Grissom, Ed White, and Roger Chaffee as they prepared for the first flight of the Apollo spacecraft. However, on Friday, January 27, during a launch rehearsal test, a fire in the command module killed the three astronauts. O'Hara says, "It was an excruciatingly difficult time. I've shared a lot of disappointments and losses with family members. In my job I took care of the whole family, so I knew them all intimately—they invited me into their lives."

Years later, O'Hara reminisced about her experience as a space nurse, saying, "I feel fortunate to have been a part of a unique and exciting time in space history."

According to Susan Kreimer, RN, a writer for NurseZone
.com (http://www.nursezone.com), there are 750
to 1,000 hyperbaric oxygen treatment centers in the
United States. Most of these are associated with
wound treatment clinics. Nurses can be credentialed
as certified hyperbaric registered nurses, as advanced
CHRNs, or as certified hyperbaric registered nurse
clinicians through certification exams developed in
conjunction with the National Board of Diving and
Hyperbaric Medical Technology (NBDHMT). The clini-
cian certification requires that an RN have a master's
degree. All requirements for certification can be found
at http://www.nbdhmt.org.

Forensic nurse. Andrea Santiago, a writer for
About.com, says that forensic nursing is a relatively
new and rapidly growing nursing specialty. It bridges
the gap between health care and law enforcement.
Nurses are trained to recognize and collect evidence
while treating patients who have been injured in
violent acts—especially victims of rape and domes-
tic violence. Most forensically trained nurses work
in, or with, hospitals, correction departments, and
jails. They may also be private consultants for law
enforcement agencies. They often work in emergency rooms, on a separate team from other emergency room staff, so that they can devote their time to
collecting evidence while caring for patients' mental
and physical needs. Forensic nurses may become
sexual assault nurse examiners (SANE) and medical legal death investigators. Most serve as expert
medical witnesses at trials.

Forensic nursing is a rapidly growing nursing subspecialty. Forensic nurses are frequently called upon to testify in trials as expert medical witnesses.

Almost all forensic nurses have master's degrees. Coursework in SANE programs focuses on the legal system, collection and preservation of evidence, providing testimony, and providing care for both the victims and the perpetrators of crime. After completing the coursework for this degree, nurses take certification exams prepared by the Commission for Forensic Nursing Certification (CFNC). This nursing specialty is fast-paced and crisis-oriented.

Nursing is a great profession, providing almost five million jobs for men and women in the United States. It pays relatively high wages, has subspecialties that fit every person's interests, and provides good job security now and for the foreseeable future. Although nursing is still considered a nontraditional career for men, it won't be for long. Nursing careers are expanding into areas that are especially appealing to men such as aviation nursing, sports nursing, and battlefield nursing.

Teens who have caring personalities, who have good work ethics, and who have a yen for challenge and adventure should strongly consider a career in nursing.

GLOSSARY

advocate To support or speak in favor of an issue or cause.

anesthetist A nurse who is trained in administering agents that abolish the sensation of pain.

assassinate To murder a politically important person.

catastrophe A sudden and very great disaster.

cerebral palsy A muscular disorder resulting from damage to the nervous system that is usually sustained at birth.

empathy The ability to share another's emotions and feelings.

ethics The study of the standards of conduct and moral judgment.

excruciating Intense or extreme pain; agonizingly painful.

facilitate To make easier or to help.

hyperbaric Characterized by greater than normal pressure as applied to gases under greater than atmospheric pressure.

Lyme disease A disease carried by ticks that causes a rash and possible nerve, heart, and joint abnormalities.

Medicaid A state and federal health program for paying certain medical expenses of persons with low incomes.

Medicare A federal health program for paying certain medical expenses of the aged.

midwife A person other than a doctor who is trained to assist at childbirth.

multiple sclerosis A disease of the central nervous system that results in loss of muscular coordination.

pinnacle The highest point or position that can be attained.

resurgence The reoccurrence or re-growth of an event or activity.

Roman candle A firework that is a long tube that shoots out balls or stars of fire one at a time.

stereotype A fixed or conventional notion or idea about something.

tuition The charge for instruction, as in a college.

FOR MORE INFORMATION

American Assembly for Men in Nursing
P.O. Box 7867
Philadelphia PA 19101-7867
(215) 243-5813
Website: http://www.aamn.org
The purpose of this organization is to provide
a framework for nurses, as a group, meet, dis-
cuss, and influence factors that affect men
as nurses.

American Association of Colleges of Nursing
One Dupont Circle NW, Suite 530
Washington, DC 20036
(202) 463-6930
Website: http://www.aacn.nche.edu
The organization is the national voice for baccalaure-
ate and graduate nursing education.

American Nurses Association
8515 Georgia Avenue, Suite 400
Silver Spring, MD 20910
(800) 274-4262
Website: http://www.nursingworld.org
The America Nurses Association fosters high standards of nursing practice, promotes the rights of
nurses in the workplace, projects positive and
realistic views of nursing, and lobbies Congress
and other regulatory agencies on health care
issues affecting nurses and the public.

Canadian Nurses Association
50 Driveway
Ottawa, ON K2P 1E2
Canada
(613) 237-2133
Website: http://www.cna-aicc.ca
The Canadian Nurses Association advances the practice and profession of nursing to improve health outcomes and strengthen Canada's publicly funded health system.

Canadian Nursing Students' Association
Fifth Avenue Court
99 Fifth Avenue, Suite 15
Ottawa, ON K1S 5K4
Canada
(613) 235-3150
Website: http://www.cnsa.ca
The Canadian Nursing Students' Association represents nursing students and their interests to government, health care organizations, and the media.

Job Corps
200 Constitution Avenue NW, Suite N4463
Washington, DC 20210
(202) 693-3000
Website: http://www.jobcorps.gov
The Job Corps is a residential career-training program where students can earn high school diplomas while training for careers in high-growth industries.

National Association for Practical Nurse Education
and Service
1940 Duke Street, Suite 200
Alexandria, VA 22314
(703) 933-1003
Website: http://napnes.org
This organization is dedicated to promoting and
defending the practice, education and regulation of
licensed practical and vocational nurses, practical
nurse educators, practical nursing schools, and
practical nursing students.

National Council of State Boards of Nursing
111 East Wacker Drive, Suite 2900
Chicago, IL 60601
(312) 525-3600
Website: http://www.ncsbn.org
This organization provides a mechanism through which
the boards of nursing of all states may act and
counsel together on matters of common interest
and concern affecting public health, safety, and wel-
fare. It also develops licensing exams in nursing.

National Network of Career Nursing Assistants
3577 Easton Road
Norton, OH 44203
(330) 825-0342
Website: http://cna-network.org
This organization is an educational organization promoting the education, research, advocacy, and peer
support development for nursing assistants in nursing homes and other long-term care settings.

National Student Nurses Association
45 Main Street, Suite 606
Brooklyn, New York 11201
(718) 210-0705
Website: http://www.nsna.org
The National Student Nurses Association mentors the
professional development of future registered nurses
and facilitates their entrance into the profession by
providing education, resources, leadership opportunities, and career guidance.

Websites

Because of the changing nature of Internet links,
Rosen Publishing has developed an online list of
websites related to the subject of this book. This
site is updated regularly. Please use this link to
access the list:

http://www.rosenlinks.com/RDFM/Nurs

FOR FURTHER READING

Alexander, Michael. *Confessions of a Male Nurse.* New York, NY: HarperCollins Publishing, 2012.

Arnoldussen, Barbara. *First Year Nurse: Wisdom, Warnings, and What I Wish I'd Known My first 100 Days on the Job.* 3rd ed. New York, NY: Kaplan Publishing, 2009.

Brown, Theresa. *Critical Care: A New Nurse Faces Death, Life, and Everything in Between.* New York, NY: HarperOne, 2011.

Calvert, Candace. *Critical Care.* Carol Stream, IL: Tyndale House Publishing, 2009.

Culp, Jennifer. *Jump-Starting a Career as Medical Assistants & Certified Nursing Assistants* (Health Care Careers in 2 Years). New York, NY: Rosen Publishing, 2014.

Fitzpatrick, Joyce, and Emerson E. Ea, eds. *201 Careers in Nursing.* New York, NY: Springer Publishing, 2011.

Freedman, Jeri. *Jump-Starting a Career in Hospitals & Home Health Care* (Health Careers in 2 Years). New York, NY: Rosen Publishing, 2014.

Hudson, Janice. *Trauma Junkie: Memoirs of an Emergency Flight Nurse.* Richmond Hill, ON, Canada: Firefly Books, 2010.

Johnson, Todd. *The Sweet By and By.* New York, NY: HarperCollins Publishers, 2009.

Kacen, Alex. *Opportunities in Allied Health Careers.* New York, NY: McGraw-Hill, 2008.

Lamb, Wally. *The Hour I First Believed.* New York, NY: Harper Perennial, 2009.

Lineberry, Cate. *The Secret Rescue: An Untold Story of American Nurses and Medics Behind Nazi Lines.* New York, NY: Little Brown and Co., 2013.

O'Lynn, Chad. *A Man's Guide to a Nursing Career.* New York, NY: Springer Publishing, 2013.

Peate, Ian. *The Student's Guide to Becoming a Nurse.* 2nd ed. Chichester, West Sussex, England: Wiley-Blackwell, 2012.

Peterson's. *Nursing Programs 2014.* Albany, NY: Peterson's Publishing, 2013.

Porter, Joy. *Start Your Health Career Faster: Become a Nursing Assistant and Get Training Reimbursed.* Seattle, WA: CreateSpace Independent Publishing, 2013.

Rogers, Kara, ed. *Medicine and Healers Through History* (Health and Disease in Society). New York, NY: Britannica Educational Publishing and Rosen Editorial Services, 2011.

Shatkin, Laurence. *10 Best College Majors for Your Personality.* Indianapolis, IN: JIST Publishing, 2011.

Shatkin, Laurence, and Michael Farr. *Top 100 Careers Without a Four-Year Degree.* 10th ed. Indianapolis, IN: JIST Publishing, 2012.

Sullivan, Eleanor. *Assumed Dead.* Buffalo, NY: Harlequin, 2010.

Trant, Kate, and Sue Usher, eds. *Nurse: Past, Present and Future: The Making of Modern Nursing.* London, England: Black Dog Publishing, 2010.

Ward, Brian. *The Story of Medicine* (A Journey Through History). New York, NY: Rosen Publishing, 2011.

BIBLIOGRAPHY

Academy of Achievement. "Biography: Naomi Judd." Retrieved December 13, 2013 (http://www .achievement.org/autodoc/page/jud0bio-1).

American Association of Colleges of Nursing. "Employment of New Nurse Graduates and Employer Preferences for Baccalaureate-Prepared Nurses." October, 2011. Retrieved October 31, 2013 (http://www.aacn.nche.edu/leading -initiative-news/news/employment-of-new-nurse -graduates-and-employer-preferences-for -baccalaureate-prepared-nurses).

American Association for the History of Nursing. "Gravesites of Prominent Nurses-Whitman." Retrieved November 3, 2013 (http://www.aahn .org/gravesites/whitman.html).

Casselman, Ben. "Is Nursing Still an Attractive Career Choice?" *Wall Street Journal*, April 25, 2013. Retrieved November 14, 2013 (http://blogs.wsj .com/economics/2013/04/25/is-nursing-still -an-attractive-career-choice).

CBS News. "Heroic Nurse, Shot 27 Times, Saved Lives." March 30, 2009. Retrieved October 30, 2013 (http://www.cbsnews.com/2100-500202 _162-4902345.html).

Conradt, Stacy. "10 Words Invented by Authors." March 24, 2010. Retrieved December 10, 2013 (http://mentalfloss.com/article/24284/10-words -invented-authors).

Brewin, Bob. "First Nurse Nominated as Army Sur- geon General," *Government Executive*, May 5,

2011. Retrieved October 25, 2013 (http://www
.govexec.com/federal-news/2011/05/first
-nurse-nominated-as-army-surgeon-general/
33918).

Friedel, Linda. "LPN Program Is Entry Point for Many
Nurses." *Kansas City Nursing News*, May 28, 2013.
Retrieved November 14, 2013 (http://www
.kcnursingnews.com/features/article_6752626e
-5e7c-5b09-94b7-d3541d186d8b.html).

International Council of Nurses. "Definition of Nursing." Retrieved October 25, 2013 (http://www.icn
.ch/about-icn/icn-definition-of-nursing).

Jaslow, Ryan. "Number of Male U.S. Nurses Triple
Since 1970." CBSNews.com, February 26, 2013.
Retrieved February 14, 2014 (http://www
.cbsnews.com/news/number-of-male-us-nurses
-triple-since-1970).

Job Corps. "LPN Training Connections." Cassadaga
Job Corps Academy. Retrieved November 14, 2013
(http://cassadaga.jobcorps.gov/Libraries/pdf/
lpn.sflb).

Kreimer, Susan. "Hyperbaric Nursing: A Growing
Specialty." *Nurse Zone*, 2008. Retrieved November
25, 2013 (http://www.nursezone.com/recent
-graduates/recent-graduates-featured-articles/
Hyperbaric-Nursing-A-Growing-Speciality_20096.aspx).

Madison College. "Cost Comparisons: Get Smart.
Save Cash." Retrieved November 21, 2013 (http://
madisoncollege.edu/cost-comparisons).

Martindale, Scott. "Intern Who Saved Rep. Giffords
Honored in Anaheim." *Orange County Register*,
June 22, 2011. Retrieved November 9, 2013

(http://www.ocregister.com/news/hernandez
-305577-health-students.html).
National Aeronautics and Space Administration.
"Meet: Dee O'Hara, First Nurse to NASA's First
Astronauts." NASA Quest Female Frontiers.
Retrieved November 24, 2013 (http://quest.arc
.nasa.gov/space/frontiers/ohara.html).
Obama, Barack. "Strengthening Our Health Care Work-
force." June 16, 2010. Retrieved October 27, 2013
(http://www.whitehouse.gov/photos-and-video/
video/strengthening-our-health-care-workforce).
Robert Wood Johnson Foundation. "The Case for
Academic Progression: Why Nurses Should Advance
Their Education and the Strategies That Make This
Feasible." September 2013. Retrieved November
14, 2013 (http://www.mass.edu/currentinit/
documents/rwjfsept2013.pdf).
Santiago, Andrea. "Forensic Nursing Careers; What
Does a Forensic Nurse Do, and How Do I Become
a Forensic Nurse?" Retrieved November 24, 2013
(http://healthcareers.about.com/od/nursingcareers/
a/ForensicNursing.html).
Stults, Kimberly. "The Definition of Nursing." *Journal of
Undergraduate Nursing*. Vol. 4, No. 1, Fall 2002.

INDEX

About the Author

Linda Bickerstaff, M.D., is a general and peripheral vascular surgeon. Early in her surgical career, she realized that excellent nursing care for her patients would be the key to her success as a surgeon and that skilled, dedicated nurses are priceless. She is grateful to the many dedicated nurses who have cared for her patients throughout the years.

Photo Credits